HOW
ABOUT
YOU?

HOW
ABOUT
YOU?

SELF-REFLEXION GUIDE
TO ACCOMPANY
LEADING THROUGH CULTURE

KEN WILCOX

Waterside Productions
Cardiff-by-the-Sea, California

Printed in the United States of America

First Printing, 2020

ISBN-13: 978-1-960583-09-3 print edition
ISBN-13: 978-1-960583-10-9 ebook edition

Waterside Productions
2055 Oxford Ave.
Cardiff-by-the-Sea, CA 92007

www.waterside.com

TABLE OF CONTENTS

CHAPTER ONE

WHY DO YOU WANT TO LEAD?

So, you want to be a leader.
Or someone else wants you to be in charge.

Do you know why you've been chosen?
Or if you haven't yet been chosen, do you know why you want to be?

Time for a little self-reflection.
Try spending some time with yourself answering these questions:

WHAT MOTIVATES YOU?

Money?

- Leaders get paid more.
- Are you targeting wealth?

Prestige?

- Are you looking for admiration, recognition, fame?

Achievement?

- Are you hoping for praise from others?
- Or a sense of accomplishment from within?

Competition?

- Do you like the feeling that you're winning?

Power or control?

- Do you really just like being in charge?

Helping others?

- Does it make you feel good to watch others grow and succeed?

Do you have a mission?

- Is there something that you want to change in order to make things better?

Once you've answered these questions on your own, you might try discussing your answers with someone who knows you well, like a close friend. Be open and honest. Ask your friend to be open and honest as well.

All of these potential motivations are common and valid.

That said, the most successful leaders—in terms of garnering the admiration, affection, and respect of other people—typically have a sense of mission. They are not content with the status quo. Rather, they want to make things happen. They want to implement changes. And the changes they want to implement usually benefit the people who are following them, not just themselves.

> *Remember: The people who agree to follow you do so voluntarily. One of the most important questions on their minds is, "How will following you benefit me?"*

So, if you have a mission, what is it? How will achieving your mission benefit your followers?

Other things to think about:

What are your best attributes?

_____

_____

_____

_____

_____

What are your least attractive behaviors?

_____

_____

_____

_____

_____

When do you exhibit your least attractive behaviors? (hungry, tired, stressed?)

_____

_____

What qualities do you lack that you need a team member to supply?

_____

_____

_____

_____

Check again with your close friend to find out if he or she thinks your self-assessment is on the mark.

Knowing these things about yourself is important, because once you are in a position of leadership, your followers are going to be copying you.

What things about you do you hope they will copy?

What things do you hope they won't?

Two other things to consider:

1. What do you like most?

    Learning things that will make you an expert?
    OR
    Teaching others the skills and knowledge you have acquired so that they, too, will become experts?
    OR
    Leading other experts in a mission that will accomplish something important and make life better for the whole organization—or at least for your entire team?

    Example:

    After two years in junior college, Sheila decided to enlist in the military. People told her that she had the personality for it but not the skill set. However, the army would teach her the skills she would need to succeed. Sheila enjoyed the two years she'd signed up for. She really liked learning.

    After two years in the army, she decided to re-up; that is, she signed up for another two.

    The people she reported to reviewed her progress. She'd done such a good job of acquiring skills that they wanted to promote her to team leader. Sheila was flattered, but she didn't want the promotion. She felt uncomfortable leading because she didn't feel that her newly acquired skills were strong enough. In short, she didn't feel she knew enough to lead. Her commanding officer suggested a compromise: instead of leading, how about instructing? Sheila became an instructor of new enlistees, helping them to acquire the skills she'd just spent two years learning.

    Perhaps in another two years, Sheila would feel better about leading.

On the other hand, some people recognize that they are uniquely skilled at training others and are content to remain in that important role. What's critical is to have the self-knowledge to understand your natural talent. If you are a leader of a talented trainer, you may want to create a compensation system that rewards him or her for these skills, rather than pushing that person into a role that does not fit his or her strengths.

2. One of the important abilities of a leader is leveraging yourself through others.

   By that, I mean that you must be able and willing to delegate tasks and, later, roles, to your team and trust that they will do as good a job as you would. This stems from your ability to set examples, build a confidence-inspiring team around yourself, create a good culture in your organization, and articulate a vision that inspires others—while leaving most decision-making and almost all the execution to your team.

What appeals to you about this? What concerns you?

_____

_____

_____

_____

_____

_____

Example:

Tyrone works in a start-up. His boss gives him an assignment. Tyrone has a choice: He can either complete the assignment himself, in which case his boss wants it finished in three months. Alternatively, his boss is willing to assign two other people to work with Tyrone on the project, creating a team of three. Tyrone will be in charge. In exchange for these additional resources, Tyrone's boss wants the project completed in one month, not three.

Tyrone prefers working alone. He doesn't feel comfortable delegating to others and holding them accountable. He's also worried that the other two people his boss will assign to him won't be as conscientious as he feels he is. Tyrone is sure he can do the job better and faster himself.

Which would you prefer? Why?

_____

_____

_____

_____

_____

_____

If Tyrone asked you for advice, what would you suggest and why?

_____

_____

_____

_____

_____

_____

For a real-life example, review the case study about Carly Fiorina in the appendix.

CHAPTER 2

YOU CAN'T DO IT ALONE

Congratulations!

You're in a leadership role and are ready to go.

One of your first tasks will be developing your leadership team.
Do you know what kinds of people you should hire around yourself?
Do you know how to choose your team and cultivate it over time?
And how do you set the tone once you have your team in place?

As leader, you must be ever mindful of not only the "health" of each individual team member, but the "health" of the team as a whole.

In other words, every team-related decision that you make as leader—choosing who to hire and why, setting the tone, looking honestly at your own behavior and how you handle situations that aren't going well—all work together to create a team that either functions in a healthy way or does not.

HOW DO YOU KNOW WHO TO HIRE?

Try answering these questions:

- What is the aptitude, skill set, and attitude of each individual team member and also of the team as a whole?

_____

_____

_____

_____

_____

_____

- Do your team members work well together, or do they try to compete with each other or sabotage things? What are examples of these behaviors?

_____

_____

_____

_____

_____

_____

- Are your team members complementary to each other? In other words, are all bases covered, or are there holes in the team that you need to fill? What are they?

_____

_____

_____

_____

_____

_____

As leader, you are responsible for selecting and coaching your team.
Your job is to make sure that your team is whole and that each team member is talented and a good fit. This is one of your most important responsibilities and can be more difficult than you suppose.

Often, there's already a team in place when a new leader comes in.
When that happens, you'll want to think about the following:

- Should you keep the team you inherit or build a new one?

- What characteristics should you be looking for in the individual members of your team?

- Since change is inevitable, how do you keep a team working well together and cultivate it over time?

A healthy team starts with the right people.

Do you like being praised? Do you gravitate toward the nicest-seeming people? So does everyone else, but that's not what you need to build the best team. Sometimes the people you most need on the team are those who will challenge you (politely).

Instead, try answering these questions:

- Are you hiring for talent, intelligence, and experience? (Hint: Hire the smartest, most talented, most experienced people you can find. There's no substitute for these characteristics.) How do you define these? How do you assess them in interviews?

_____

_____

_____

_____

_____

_____

- What are your (and your team's) strengths and weaknesses?

_____

_____

_____

_____

_____

_____

- What kinds of people/types of skills must you find to balance out gaps where you and your team lack certain strengths or skill sets?

  _____

  _____

  _____

  _____

  _____

  _____

- Are your team members different in ways that create a vibrant, cohesive whole? (Hint: Avoid people who frequently tell you how great you and/or they are. Hire people who complement [not compliment] you and the rest of your team.)

  _____

  _____

  _____

  _____

  _____

  _____

Thinking about the qualities of your team: On the spectrum of human behavior, you'll find passive-aggressive people at one end and obnoxiously assertive people at the other. Passive-aggressive people always agree with you, so you tend to think of them as smart and cooperative—until you find that they've been bad-mouthing you behind your back and going underground, seeking to undermine decisions. Obnoxiously assertive people are hard to miss: they're loud and annoying and openly fight leadership and oppose decisions. Aim for hiring adult-to-adult people, who are right in the middle of the spectrum and know how to speak their minds and disagree constructively.)

- Think about the people on your team and also people from your life experience. Who do you see as passive-aggressive? Adult-to-adult? Obnoxiously assertive? Why? (It's fine not to use real names here.) How have you interacted with them?

_____

_____

_____

_____

_____

_____

- Are you hiring people with emotional IQ, who are capable of working with others on an adult-to-adult basis? How do you assess this quality in an interview?

_____

_____

_____

_____

_____

_____

- What are your values?

_____

_____

_____

_____

_____

_____

- What values are important for your team to share?

_____

_____

_____

_____

_____

_____

• Are you hiring for values (broad statements of belief about proper conduct)? How do you identify these?

_____

_____

_____

_____

_____

_____

_____

_____

Remember: All of your team members should have the same values. Although it's difficult finding people with similar values, it's worth it. Under any circumstances, keep searching until you find them—or at least find people with values similar enough that they could accept/embrace the differences on an adult-to-adult basis.

Here's a good strategy for hiring people with the same values:
While interviewing, pose situations where there would be more than one possible course of action, so the people have to think about it on the spot. See what they say. Their answers will be revealing.

Write down some situations that you could describe to a potential team member during an interview to see how they will answer:

_____

_____

_____

_____

_____

_____

If you can, convene some of your team members to role-play these interviews.

Now consider the following:

- Are you hiring for core capabilities, not just previous title?
- What are the candidate's interests and inherent skills? (Circle all that apply.)

   Analyzing
   Problem-solving
   Selling
   Negotiating
   Teaching
   Leading people (as opposed to managing them)
   Managing people
   Managing things or projects
   Consulting (providing expertise in a persuasive and helpful manner)

Now think about yourself and write down some examples of times that you have engaged in these activities and how you felt about doing them:

_____

_____

_____

_____

_____

_____

- Which of the following do you enjoy, and which are you good at? (Circle all that apply.)

   Managing people
   Leading people

Managing tasks
Analyzing things
Teaching others about things I've analyzed
Selling things
Negotiating
Consulting
Problem-solving

- Are you hiring for diversity?

  Diversity is not just defined along racial, ethnic, age, and gender lines; it also means an individual's personality and interests.
  Conformity (except to certain specific values) is not just unimportant; it should be actively discouraged. Otherwise, you'll end up losing your most creative team members.

Consider these questions and write your answers below:

- What are your beliefs about qualities you should look for in assembling your team?

  _____

  _____

  _____

  _____

  _____

- What gaps exist in the skills and attitudes you need in your team?

  _____

  _____

  _____

  _____

  _____

  _____

- What might you need to rethink and change in forming your team?

_____

_____

_____

_____

_____

_____

- What are you best at, and what do you enjoy doing? With this in mind, what kind of people do you need to hire around yourself to complement your natural skill set and create a diverse, vibrant team?

_____

_____

_____

_____

_____

_____

- Are you hiring someone because you like them or because they are what you and your team actually need?

_____

_____

_____

_____

_____

_____

Remember: Be very careful to hire people with values similar to your own.

SETTING THE TONE

As leader, you need to set the tone for your team and organization.
But certain dynamics can make this difficult.
People generally don't like being told what to do. And there's a part of every person that doesn't want a boss and rebels against authority figures.

So, what can you do once you've made your best effort to hire the right people?

Encourage your team members to tell you when they disagree with you.

Answer the following questions:

- How do you feel when people disagree with you? How do you act?

_____

_____

_____

_____

_____

_____

- Is this a helpful response? Why or why not?

_____

_____

_____

_____

_____

_____

- Might any part of your reaction be related to a previous dynamic in your life, rather than the current situation that you and your team are working through? Explain. What might you do to address this?

  _____

  _____

  _____

  _____

  _____

  _____

- Are you genuinely approachable? What makes you think so?

  _____

  _____

  _____

  _____

  _____

  _____

- Do you encourage others to state their opinions and take time to consider the merit in the opinions being offered?

  _____

  _____

  _____

  _____

  _____

  _____

- What do your answers to the questions above say about the value you place on setting the tone for your organization?

_____

_____

_____

_____

_____

_____

_____

_____

Remember: Constructive disagreement is helpful. The last thing you want is to be surrounded by a bunch of yes-men who won't tell you the truth.

Take a few minutes and think about these questions:

- Do you encourage others to state their opinions? How do you respond when they do? Do you listen thoughtfully or immediately disagree with them?

_____

_____

_____

_____

_____

- Do you take time to consider the merit in opinions being offered and praise their positive aspects? How can you show team members that you appreciate their contributions?

_____

_____

_____

_____

_____

_____

---

*Remember: Seeing the merit in another's opinion
does not bind you to accept it as your own. But it
may help you make a better decision. Ultimately, as
leader, it's your job to make the final decision and be
responsible for it. A very helpful response can be to
say, "Let me think about that and get back to you."
Saying No is our natural default to anything new
and challenging. It's amazing the number of times
that an automatic "No" can become a "Yes if…"
upon consideration. This approach provides "wins"
on several dimensions: your team members feel heard
and appreciated; you receive more frequent and often
helpful suggestions; and you may find unanticipated
aptitudes among your staff, which can help you direct
their trajectories in more productive ways.*

Take a few minutes and answer the following questions:

- What do you do now to set the tone for your team, unit, or organization?

_____

_____

_____

_____

_____

_____

• How has that been effective/ineffective?

_____

_____

_____

_____

_____

_____

• What might you do differently to set a better tone?

_____

_____

_____

_____

_____

_____

• How do you plan to deal with resistance, disagreement, reluctance to speak, or other obstacles you encounter in setting a different tone?

_____

_____

_____

_____

_____

_____

Be creative! One firm-founding venture capitalist was known as a man of "decided opinions" but wanted to be sure he received his team's unvarnished input on investment decisions. As a result, he instituted a rule that every investment professional would express their opinion on a deal with the most junior person going first.

What if you make the wrong decision?
Even the best leaders make mistakes. What separates the good from the great is the willingness to make the hard decisions—even if wrong in retrospect—and:

- Admit to them.

- Live with the consequences?

- Learn from them.

Answer this question:

- What will you do when you make a decision that turns out to be wrong?

_____

_____

_____

_____

_____

_____

A word on turnover
Change is inevitable, and therefore so is turnover. Situations and people can change over time. A team evolves and, with it, people's roles.

So, what do you do if a team member is not working out?
Ask yourself:

- What are this person's primary skills?

_____

_____

_____

_____

_____

_____

• What skills does this job require?

_____

_____

_____

_____

_____

_____

• Is this person in the wrong job?

_____

_____

_____

_____

_____

_____

• Can we solve this mismatch with coaching? Or would a different role better utilize their skills?

_____

_____

_____

_____

_____

_____

A common mistake is to promote someone who is a good manager of people into a leadership position without trying to figure out if they actually have the qualities of a good leader.

Sometimes it works, sometimes it doesn't.

If it doesn't, it's usually because that person lacks the vision and communication skills necessary to motivate large groups of people.

Good people managers and good leaders are two different things.

If you have a problem with a team member:

- Try coaching first.
- If that doesn't work, you may have to fire someone.
- If you do have to fire someone, remember: At a certain level, you're doing them a favor—releasing them from a place where they don't fit so they can find a place where they do.

If you're not sure about a potential team member, it's generally better to delay a hiring decision a little longer than to bring someone on board who won't work out. But if you do make that mistake, correct it as soon as you realize that you've chosen someone who is not going to make it.

SEPARATING FROM STAFF

Sometimes, despite your best efforts, you find that you'll need to separate from an employee, both for their good and your organization's. When you do have to fire someone, ask yourself:

- What do you do when you discover that you have hired or inherited someone who belongs in another organization, but not yours?

_____

_____

_____

_____

_____

_____

- How do you release a person without degrading them?

_____

_____

_____

_____

_____

_____

- Rather than reading them a laundry list of their shortcomings, how will you stick with your original reason, that the fit is not good, and not deviate from it?

_____

_____

_____

_____

_____

_____

- How do you enable people to leave with dignity?

_____

_____

_____

_____

_____

_____

CHAPTER 3:

BUILDING A GREAT CULTURE

As leader, your two most important tasks are:

- Building the leadership team.
- Building the culture.

Think seriously about the following questions and write your answers below:

- How do you want the people in your organization to treat each other?

_____

_____

_____

_____

_____

_____

- What will be the "rules of engagement"?

_____

_____

_____

_____

_____

_____

I believe that culture always trumps strategy. So, what's the difference?

- **Strategy** is your longer-term game plan. It speaks to the mind.
- **Culture** is the sense of knowing what it means to live/work in your company or tribe or group. It speaks to the heart.

In my experience, the heart drives the mind more than the other way around. Culture is all about how we treat each other and how we work together.

WHAT IT MEANS TO WORK HERE

Everything that happens in an organization is a result of its culture.

Before you can consciously build a culture, you must know the following things about yourself. Consider these questions and write your answers below:

- Who are you?

_____

_____

_____

_____

_____

_____

- What are your values?

_____

_____

_____

_____

_____

_____

- What values would you like your team to emulate?

_____

_____

_____

_____

_____

_____

_____

_____

*Remember: Be who you want your team members to
be, and the rest will take care of itself.*

_____

A WORD ABOUT CULTURE

Whether people like their coworkers and boss is ultimately a question of culture. People like working with others who share their values. They like reporting to people with similar values and good leadership skills.

People are happiest when they feel they belong. A place where they belong is one that reflects values similar to their own.

Think of some places and situations in your life where you felt that you genuinely belonged. List them below.

_____

_____

_____

_____

_____

_____

What was it about those situations and places that made you feel that way? Are there aspects of these qualities that you could bring to the culture and organization that you are now leading?

_____

_____

_____

_____

_____

_____

Building a culture is, in large measure, creating a set of norms that people conform to. Mainly, people know what it means to be a member of your team.

Answer the following questions:

- What does it mean to be a member of your team?

_____

_____

_____

_____

_____

_____

How can you cultivate values in your organization and create a culture that helps point all your team members in the right direction, helping them feel that they belong and know where they stand?

_____

_____

_____

_____

_____

_____

• Do you think that your team members currently feel this way? Why or why not?

_____

_____

_____

_____

_____

If you think critically about these questions, it will help you create an atmosphere of trust and loyalty among your team members.

THE VALUE OF VALUES

Values give an organization a unique sense of identity.
Values are the glue that holds a team and an organization together.

Values allow an organization to become more or less self-governing. They are the "voice of the conscience" that enables your employees/team members to know what to do, even when you or another leadership team member are not there to tell them.

I once participated in a group exercise presented by a former CEO of Silicon Valley Bank. The results were so powerful, I'd like to share that exercise with you now. Try this with your own team.

1. Identify the top employees in your hierarchy. (When we did this exercise, we identified fifty top employees in our large company.)

2. Put them in a room together.

3. Divide them into small teams (up to four or five people per team). Give each team its own table.

4. On each table, place a set of about 150 small pieces of paper that are each printed with a noun describing a virtue: "trust," "dependability," "sincerity," etc. (See Appendix 2 for a sample)

5. Have each team group the papers into piles of concepts that are similar. (Each table will probably end up with about ten to twelve piles.)

6. Ask each team to pick the five or six piles containing the concepts they'd most like to have define their culture. In each case, have them identify a single word that exemplifies each pile.

7. Using a moderator, ask all the groups to work together to build a list of eight values they can agree on.

8. Ask them to summarize the eight chosen values into a single phrase. Example: "Work hard, take responsibility, and treat each other well."

Ask yourself:

• What are the six to eight key values reflected in the culture of your company, unit, or team?

_____

_____

_____

_____

_____

• How would others in your company, unit, or team describe the culture they experience?

_____

_____

_____

_____

_____

_____

- To what extent does this culture reflect your values and the values you want your team members to emulate?

_____

_____

_____

_____

_____

_____

- What discrepancies exist between the values you espouse and the culture you now have? What needs to change to get or keep them aligned?

_____

_____

_____

_____

_____

_____

Fear or "Love"?

Richard Nixon once said: "People react to fear, not love. They don't teach that in Sunday school, but it's true."

In my experience, nothing could be further from the truth. People operating in an atmosphere of fear become:

- less creative, and then

- more protective, less open, and more "political".

Employees respond much more productively to encouragement.

Fear may work better with some people, but I'm not sure those are the ones you want in your organization.

SCHOOLS OF GOVERNANCE: COPS AND ROBBERS VS. THE VOICE OF THE CONSCIENCE

Cops and Robbers: People governing in this style believe the world consists of two types of people: responsible leaders and employees/subjects who will try to get away with anything they can for personal gain. This view leads to suspicion, micromanagement, expectations of failure, and generally poor performance by the employees who are being viewed and managed with these low expectations.

Voice of the Conscience: People governing in this style believe that the organization's norms must be ingrained in everyone, regardless of role. A foundation of values is cultivated in all team members, establishing the norms that lead to a productive and encouraging culture, so people know how to act and use good judgment even when management is not there to advise or guide them.

THINKING HORIZONTALLY

What does it mean to think horizontally? How about vertically?

Think back on your life.

Have you ever worked or lived in a place with dysfunctional dynamics? Were there passive-aggressive or obnoxiously assertive people there? Did some people act superior, as if they were in some way the "parents" who felt they needed to monitor everything going on and hold the "children" accountable, punishing them accordingly?

If this dynamic sounds familiar, I am betting that you were in an organization or situation that operated in a vertical style, with criticisms and edicts making their way (often unpleasantly) down the chain of command.

Is this a dynamic that you want to repeat in the organization you're leading? Probably not.

Thinking horizontally is actually much better for you and your team.

Thinking horizontally means that you want adults on your team who will treat those around them like adults and expect them to behave the same way. This means no "children," no "parents," no passive-aggressive people, and no obnoxiously assertive people.

But how do you achieve this?

The most important thing you can do is hire people who:

- are all intelligent; and
- come from diverse backgrounds and so bring a wide variety of experiences; and
- know how to work collaboratively on an adult-to-adult basis.

If you do this, you can't help but succeed.

Many organizations, and many managers within organizations, don't actually know how to work together collaboratively with other teams.

Collaborating means two things:

1. Knowing how to work together on an adult-to-adult basis with members of your own team.

2. Knowing how to work together successfully with other teams and business units.

Think for a moment: Deliberately or inadvertently, do you and/or some of your managers encourage competition between functional areas and even between groups within functional areas in your organization? Many managers do this. Can you think of some examples of this happening in your organization, or of people who seem to encourage this kind of behavior? List them here.

_____

_____

_____

_____

_____

_____

Many people in business think it's important to have internal groups competing against each other.

I think that's a terrible idea.

With this kind of competitive incentive structure, most people will do what the money dictates, regardless of whether their behavior benefits anyone other than themselves.

Consider:

- Is that really what you want for your organization?
- Does this align with the values you listed in chapter 2 of this workbook?

When divisions work together, no single function should dominate.

Instead, as leader, strive to build a culture in which almost everyone can see the big picture and the need for balance within it. This kind of culture is essential to optimizing any large organization.

So, how do you do this?
Implement the concept of cross-functional teams. This means that teams come together, often spontaneously, to help a client or to solve a larger problem.

Encourage managers to make decisions based on what's best for the whole corporation and accordingly the shareholders—not what's best for the managers or their individual functional areas.

In short, charge each manager with the responsibility of making decisions as if they were CEO. And require everyone to make decisions as if they were CEO for the benefit of all of your constituencies.

Have every member of your organization think about the following:

- What's best for the organization?
- For the customer?
- For the employees?
- For the shareholder?

Now, what can you do to reward this kind of behavior when you see it happening? List some ideas here.

_____

_____

_____

_____

_____

_____

IMPORTANT QUESTIONS

- Does my organization operate on a horizontal or vertical basis?

_____

_____

_____

_____

_____

_____

- How will I work on assembling and engaging cross-functional teams?

_____

_____

_____

_____

_____

_____

THE ROLE OF RESPONSIBILITY

When you make a mistake, is it enough to admit it and take the blame?

No doubt about it—doing so is critical. However, I think that is the lowest level of accepting responsibility. This sounds like: "I'll admit, I did it and I did it wrong. I wish I'd done it differently. I'll take the blame."

The highest level of accepting responsibility requires some action as well. Strive for the highest level and encourage your team and employees to do the same. This sounds like: "I'll admit, I did it and I did it wrong. I wish I'd done it differently. I'll take the blame and I will take responsibility for fixing it!"

Ask yourself:

- As leader, when someone comes to you and exhibits varying levels of accepting responsibility, how will you react?

_____

_____

_____

_____

_____

_____

- How would you wish to be treated in a situation where you made a mistake?

_____

_____

_____

_____

_____

_____

- How will you recognize or reward someone who meets the highest level of accepting responsibility?

_____

_____

_____

_____

_____

_____

- Do you take responsibility for all of your actions and decisions? Does everyone in your organization do the same?

_____

_____

_____

_____

_____

_____

THE SPECTRUM OF HUMAN BEHAVIOR

Imagine a spectrum, with combative people at one end and obsequious people at the other. Obnoxiously assertive people are at one end: they bully their way to victory. Passive-aggressive people are at the other end of the spectrum: they allow themselves to be bullied by obnoxiously assertive people. They nod and smile and agree during a meeting, but later in the hallway, they whisper about what jerks the obnoxiously assertive people are and what a bad decision you've just made.

In the middle of the spectrum—and these are the people you want on your team—are the adult-to-adult people. They are neither obnoxiously assertive nor passive-aggressive. They express themselves in meetings, sharing with the group their opinions, experience, and wisdom in a mature way. They neither dominate nor defer but are open to other people's ideas.

Have you experienced these different kinds of people in your life? Write some examples of each type that you recall below (you don't need to use people's real names—the important thing is that you really think about it).

_____

_____

_____

_____

_____

What effect do you think these different people's behavior had on you and on the group or organization that you're thinking about? Did they make the team effort harder or easier to fulfill? Which of those dynamics would you want in your own organization? Why or why not?

_____

_____

_____

_____

_____

_____

DOGSLEDS VS. ORCHESTRAS

I once met a military man from Denmark who spent his days patrolling Greenland by dogsled. He said that although from a distance a dogsled team seems happily engaged in a group effort, underneath it all a strict hierarchy exists among the dogs, and each wants to advance to the point that they must be tethered at safe distances from each other at night to keep them from killing each other in their effort to climb the hierarchy.

You would not believe how many groups operate like dogs on a dogsled team! Have you ever experienced this dynamic? Does a "dogsled" dynamic exist in the organization you lead? What makes you think so (or not)?

_____

_____

_____

_____

_____

_____

Many leaders actually encourage this "dogsled" model, incorrectly believing that it brings out the best in each participant.

Actually, this kind of model creates an unpleasant atmosphere of constant fear. And no one is at their best in that kind of stressful environment.

Solving complex problems requires many different skill sets and a high level of collaboration. For this reason, the "orchestra" style is a better model for most organizations to follow.

In an orchestra, every member is important and necessary. Each musician is unique, and all are required.

When all members of an orchestra play in harmony from the same score, they produce beautiful music together.

Ask yourself:

- Do I have a "dogsled" or an "orchestra" culture in my organization? Is that what I want? If not, what will I do to change it?

_____

_____

_____

_____

_____

A NOTE ON SUBCULTURES

How can you avoid the development of dangerous subcultures in an organization?

A good leader must work around the year, around the clock, on the culture of the entire organization, to make sure that the organization as a whole is focused on the big picture.

Otherwise, dangerous subcultures will begin to develop and will sabotage the leadership's effort to keep the organization focused on the main constituency—the customer.

Subcultures can arise in at least three different ways:

1. When a manager, usually inexperienced, goes into the "heart of darkness" and sets up their own kingdom apart from that of the corporation, building a culture of their own. This kind of manager prioritizes allegiance to their team over allegiance to fellow managers; that is, over the rest of the organization. Does "if you support me, I will support you" sound familiar? This kind of manager creates a "superior" little tribe that in time develops its own culture and starts to run roughshod over the other teams.

2. A subculture can arise in a distant place when an organization grows, expands, and sets up branches. Have you ever heard of "headquarters syndrome"? This happens when branches think that headquarters doesn't understand the unique conditions under which they're operating, while headquarters thinks the branches have "gone native" and are self-centered, considering only their own best interest. Soon the branches have their own culture. How do you solve this problem? Pull the branch manager into the organization as a whole, and encourage him or her to bond with their fellow managers from headquarters and vice versa.

3. When a company hires a number of people from another company all at the same time. The new group can bring their own culture with them and firmly believe that their culture is better than the one they're expected to join. This kind of group can cause problems for the rest of the teams through their superior attitude, lack of interest in assimilation, and refusal to compromise.

Think carefully about the following questions and write your answers below:

What kind of person are you? What are your values? What values would you like your team to emulate? How will you use your answers to the three questions above to build a positive culture in your organization?

_____

_____

_____

_____

_____

_____

Does everyone in your organization know what it means to be a member of your team and whether they belong?

_____

_____

_____

_____

_____

_____

Do you have any problems with subcultures in your organization? What will you do to improve the situation?

_____

_____

_____

_____

_____

_____

BUILDING TRUST IN YOUR TEAM

A group of people who trust each other will get a lot more done than a group of people who don't.

What causes people to trust or mistrust each other?

Trust is a primary characteristic of great organizations—in the management team and, by extension, permeating the entire organization.

So, how do you generate and grow trust?

Groups can certainly talk about it, but only individuals can put the ball into play.

At Silicon Valley Bank, we generated The Magic 12 ways to create and cultivate an atmosphere of trust within a circle of colleagues.

If you succeed, this circle of trust will, in time, spread to the entire organization. When it does, everyone will feel safer, be happier, and work more effectively.

Please be aware, these look easy. In practice, they're harder than they look.

THE MAGIC 12

1. Express yourself clearly and often. Say what you think. Show genuine interest in the ideas of others. Encourage people to approach discussions with others, displaying this same attitude.

2. Be consistent. Say the same thing every time you speak. Don't contradict yourself. In that way, you'll become predictable. *If you change your mind, be clear, open, and honest.* Say "you've heard me say X about Y. I've been thinking about it over time and I've realized I was wrong. Instead, I now think M about Y." *Solicit opinions. You can always learn from others. When you ask someone's opinion, three things will happen: They'll think you're smarter than they would otherwise; they'll like you; and they'll trust you.*

3. Solicit opinions. You can always learn from others. When you ask someone's opinion, three things will happen: They'll think you're smarter than they would otherwise; they'll like you; and they'll trust you.

4. Demonstrate respect. Don't tell people they're wrong. Even if you disagree, at

the very least, compliment them on sharing an opinion that you find interesting and that you'd like to think about more. You can always learn from opinions you disagree with.

5. Assume innocence.

6. Skip the agenda. Try as often as possible to have a conversation without an agenda. Try to go through an entire conversation without defending your own point of view.

7. Demonstrate relevant vulnerability. When you're in doubt, admit it. Don't try to seem infallible.

8. Let others decide. You don't have to make every decision yourself. In fact, if you do, you'll deny your employees and team members the opportunity to practice decision-making within parameters.

9. Show support. Support other people's decisions, even if they're below you in the pecking order.

10. Hire adults. Avoid the extreme points on the spectrum of human behavior. Act like an adult and treat others like adults.

11. Control your inner demons. We all have inner demons that rise up and try to control us when we're feeling insecure. Put a leash on yours!

12. Observe the 9th Guiding Principle, which is: "If you have an issue with another colleague, talk to him or her about it directly; do not discuss it with third parties"—unless you need coaching on how to address an issue with the person in question, and only if you actually go on to discuss it with that person.

Ask yourself:

How will you use the Magic 12 ways to create and cultivate an atmosphere of trust in your organization?

_____

_____

_____

_____

_____

_____

INVITE OTHERS TO JOIN YOU
IN DEVELOPING YOUR THOUGHTS

In conclusion, here's an effective way to develop your thoughts.

When grappling with a problem, I may spend several days thinking about it in conversation with others, either individually or in small groups of two or three. I find that this works much better than sitting alone in my office, trying to solve a problem by myself.

Want to try it? Here's how:

Keep lots of flip charts in your office and record your thought process as it evolves over time. Bring in a member of your team—say, Bob—who's pretty smart and knows a lot about the topic. Describe the problem (pictorially, using flip charts if possible). Ask Bob's opinion on various aspects of the problem. Write his opinion down on one of the flip charts.

After the conversation, when Bob has left the room, look at the flip charts and ruminate. Reformulate your theory (point of view) based on Bob's input and your thoughts on it.
Later in the day, invite another team member—say, Sharon—to come and talk with you about it. Do the same things again.

Repeat the process over the next several days with various other people.

In a matter of days, you'll develop a point of view that's much more sophisticated and closer to a real solution than your original viewpoint.

Advantages of this approach include:

- You and your team members will enjoy it.

- Your team members will feel respected and appreciated.

- Since team members have input into the finished product and a sense of what's going on, you'll already have achieved some buy-in for your ultimate decision.

- This approach builds trust among the members of your leadership team.

Remember: All groups have a culture, whether they know it or not. And some cultures are more encouraging and productive than others.

To help define an effective work culture, consider these questions with your colleagues:

- Do the people in your organization know what it means to work there?

- Do they know and understand the significance of your organization's values?

- Do you rely on a "cops and robbers" mechanism to ensure proper behavior, or do you attempt to instill in each of your people a "voice of the conscience"?

- Does your leadership motivate through fear or encouragement?

- Are you more "vertical" or "horizontal"? That is, do you and your colleagues spend more time managing up and down, or do you spend more time managing sideways (building working relationships with peers)?

- Do you and your colleagues deal with disagreement in an adult-to-adult fashion, or do you vacillate between being obnoxiously assertive and passive-aggressive?

- Is your organization more like a dogsled or an orchestra? Why?

- Do you have subcultures? Are they productive or destructive? How do you deal with them?

- How high is the level of trust in your organization, and what could you do to improve it?

Ask yourself:

- Do the people in your organization trust each other? How do you know?

_____

_____

_____

_____

_____

_____

- Do you demonstrate respect and solicit other people's opinions?

_____

_____

_____

_____

_____

_____

- How will you use the 9th Guiding Principle to improve the trust culture throughout your organization?

_____

_____

_____

_____

_____

_____

A good example of how *not* to create a cluture of trust is Jeffrey Skilling and the culture he created at Enron. See Appendix 1 for a profile of the company and hisrole.

CHAPTER 4

THE VISION THING

"The Vision Thing" is not well understood by most people. It's seldom talked about, either in the media or in everyday life among friends and acquaintances. And yet, it is perhaps the most important aspect of leadership, as it ensures that everyone is pointed in the right direction.

- How would you describe the meaning of the word "vision"?

_____

_____

_____

_____

_____

"Purpose"—another important concept—is closely related to "vision."

- How would you describe the meaning of the word "purpose"?

_____

_____

_____

_____

_____

• How do vision and purpose relate to each other?

_____

_____

_____

_____

_____

_____

Think about leaders you have either known or at least known about. Pick one or two whom you have personally experienced through an organization that you've been part of—perhaps a for-profit company, or perhaps a not-for-profit company. Or perhaps a sports team. Or maybe a church. Try to pick a leader (or leaders) whom you respect, or at least one or two whom others respect.

In each case, what was their vision? And what was the purpose of the organization they were leading, as they described it?

• Pupose:

_____

_____

_____

_____

_____

• Vision:

_____

_____

_____

_____

_____

_____

- How good was this leader at articulating the purpose? At articulating the vision? What could he or she have done better?

_____

_____

_____

_____

_____

_____

1. Did the leader's vision appeal to you? Did you find it compelling?

   - Why or why not?

_____

_____

_____

_____

_____

_____

2. Let's stay with one or two of these leaders for a while.

   - What were their values? (List at least three.)

_____

_____

_____

_____

_____

_____

- How did you know what their values were? Did they talk about them? Or did they exemplify them in the way that they acted? Or both?

_____

_____

_____

_____

_____

_____

- How did you feel about their values?

_____

_____

_____

_____

_____

- Were their values like your own?

_____

_____

_____

_____

_____

_____

3. How would you define "strategy" and "tactics"? What are the differences?

_____

_____

_____

_____

_____

4. Let's go back to one or the other of the leaders you've chosen for this exercise. What were they best at?

    •   Purpose?
    •   Vision?
    •   Values?
    •   Strategy?
    •   Tactics?

    And what were they worst at?

_____

_____

_____

_____

_____

5. Now, let's take a look at yourself as a leader. Which of these five things do you think you are best at?

_____

_____

_____

_____

_____

_____

- Why?

_____

_____

_____

_____

_____

_____

- Worst at?

_____

_____

_____

_____

- Why?

_____

_____

_____

_____

_____

_____

6. Think about your favorite boss. And think about your worst boss. I'm just talking about your immediate boss, not the CEO or top leader of the organization. Was your boss good at describing what the top leaders of your organization said about the purpose and vision of your organization and their vision of what life would look like once your organization achieved its purpose?

7. Again, think about your bosses, both the good ones and the bad ones. Do (did) they do a good job of describing the values of the organization? How about the strategy of the organization? Do they do a good job of helping you understand what they expected you personally to achieve?

Most importantly, do they tell you *what* they want you to achieve?
OR:
Do they tell you *how* they want you to achieve what they want you to achieve?

• Do you think it makes a difference?

_____

_____

_____

_____

_____

_____

8. Imagine an organization that you might like to be a part of, or perhaps even lead. Describe it in terms of:

• Purpose

_____

_____

_____

_____

_____

_____

- Vision

_____

_____

_____

_____

_____

- Values

_____

_____

_____

_____

_____

- Strategy

_____

_____

_____

_____

- Tactics: For the most part, let's leave tactics up to the people who are actually doing the work on the front lines.

But there are some times that a leader will have to step in. For instance, Travis Kalanick, the founder and CEO of Uber, had a grand vision of disrupting the taxi industry by democratizing short-distance car transportation. His tactics of "move fast and break things" may have worked when dealing with the entrenched bureaucracy around the taxi industry, but he later overreached, restructuring the company ownership to give himself super-voting power and being caught on video castigating a driver with foul language. The board here had clearly lost control of their CEO and should have stepped in long before to rein in Kalanick's behavior—his tactics—which had crossed the line into abuse.

CHAPTER 5

MAKING AND EXECUTING ON GREAT DECISIONS— CYRUS THE GREAT

Think about leaders you have known or at least observed in your company or in some other organization you've been a part of.

How do they go about making big decisions?

Do they involve others in their decision-making process? Or do they make decisions by themselves without consulting others?

1. If they involve others, how do you think they involve them?

   • By discussing the relevant issues with them in a group setting?

   • By discussing the relevant issues with them one-on-one?

   • By voting?

   • By attempting to reach consensus?

2. What are the advantages and disadvantages of each of these approaches?

   • Making big decisions by themselves and then announcing them?

   _____

   _____

   _____

_____

_____

_____

- Discussing relevant issues with others before making a decision?

  - In a group setting

_____

_____

_____

_____

_____

_____

  - One-on-one?

_____

_____

_____

_____

_____

_____

  - Voting?

_____

_____

_____

_____

_____

_____

• Trying to achieve consensus?

_____

_____

_____

_____

_____

_____

3. Think about your work experience. Have you ever been part of a group/depart-ment/team that lost its leader? (Meaning the leader either left of their own accord or was asked to leave.) When upper-level management replaced the missing lead-er, where did they look for a replacement?

    • Within the group/department/team? Elsewhere in the organization? Or in the market?

    _____

    _____

    _____

    _____

    _____

    _____

    • What qualities did they look for in the new leader? Subject matter expertise? Or management/leadership ability?

    _____

    _____

_____

_____

_____

_____

- Which do you think is more important? Why?

_____

_____

_____

_____

_____

_____

4. As an organization grows in size, is it possible for the person at the top to make all of the major decisions alone?

- If yes, with or without input from others?

_____

_____

_____

_____

_____

- If not, why not?

_____

_____

_____

_____

_____

_____

- If you believe that the leader will ultimately have to delegate some decision-making to others, why do you believe that?

_____

_____

_____

_____

_____

- And how should they do it?

_____

_____

_____

_____

_____

- What does it mean to "delegate within parameters"?

_____

_____

_____

_____

_____

_____

- If the leader doesn't like a decision made by a subordinate to whom they have delegated the power to make the decision, what should they do?

_____

_____

_____

_____

_____

_____

5. Let's talk about the "4-D" decision-making process (discuss, decide, deliver, debrief).

- Would you utilize it?

_____

_____

_____

_____

_____

- Why or why not?

_____

_____

_____

_____

_____

_____

- When would you use it?

_____

_____

_____

_____

_____

_____

- When wouldn't you use it?

_____

_____

_____

_____

_____

_____

- What are the challenges in implementing it?

_____

_____

_____

_____

_____

• And how would you address those challenges? (i.e., What rules would you put in place to make sure, for yourself and for others, that this process works?)

_____

_____

_____

_____

_____

_____

6. Do you think that most disagreements stem from misunderstandings? Or from different points of view?

• To the extent that they stem from misunderstandings, what causes these misunderstandings?

_____

_____

_____

_____

_____

_____

• What would you recommend to help avoid misunderstandings?

_____

_____

_____

_____

_____

_____

7. If you were in charge, how would you go about trying to resolve conflicts between people who report to you?

   • If the conflict appeared to stem from misunderstanding?

   _____

   _____

   _____

   _____

   _____

   _____

   • If the conflict appeared to stem from differences in perspective?

   _____

   _____

   _____

   _____

   _____

   _____

8. Many people say that meetings are a waste of time.

   • Are they?

   _____

   _____

   _____

_____

_____

_____

- If not, why not?

_____

_____

_____

_____

_____

- What can the person in charge do to help ensure that meetings are effective?

_____

_____

_____

_____

_____

- In terms of preparation?

_____

_____

_____

_____

_____

- In terms of ground rules?

_____

_____

_____

_____

_____

_____

- In terms of methods and procedures?

_____

_____

_____

_____

_____

_____

- In terms of follow-up?

_____

_____

_____

_____

_____

_____

CHAPTER 6

COMMUNICATING WITH YOUR CONSTITUENCIES

As leader, you are responsible for communicating with your organization's constituencies—all of your employees, your customers, the community, the government, regulators, and so on. You may not do all of the communicating yourself, but you are still responsible for ensuring that it takes place.

1. Assuming you've been a member of an organization—whether a business or some other kind of entity—think for a moment about how the leadership there communicated with its constituencies, particularly its employees/members.

    - Did you feel it was enough?

    _____

    _____

    _____

    _____

    _____

    _____

    - Did you think it was timely (meaning soon enough)?

    _____

    _____

_____

_____

_____

_____

- Did you find it helpful/reassuring? Why or why not?

_____

_____

_____

_____

_____

_____

- What could the leadership have done to improve communications?

_____

_____

_____

_____

_____

_____

2. What kind of communicator are you?
   Do you like telling others what's on your mind? Do you often wonder things like:

   - What do the people who work with/for me want to know? (Not just _need_ to know, but also _want_ to know.)

_____

_____

_____

_____

_____

_____

- What do they worry about?

_____

_____

_____

_____

_____

_____

- Will they feel more secure or confident if I share more information with them?

_____

_____

_____

_____

_____

- Do I willingly share information? Or do I typically withhold information?

  - If I typically withhold information, what makes me do this? How can I change?

  _____

  _____

  _____

_____

_____

_____

- And would my employees benefit from knowing more than I typically share? How would they benefit? If I continue to withhold information, will not knowing what's going on cause my employees to worry unnecessarily? Is there any downside to telling them more?

_____

_____

_____

_____

_____

_____

3. Now ask yourself these questions:

- When I'm working on solving a problem, do I try to solve it myself, or do I involve others?

- Do I typically think things through by myself or by conversing with others?

- Am I comfortable getting input from others when I'm in the middle of solving a problem, or do I prefer to solve it by myself and then announce the solution to others?

- If I'm more inclined to solve problems by myself, when I find a solution, do I usually make a special point of sharing the solution with others? Or do I sometimes forget to tell others that I've found a solution and what it is?

- If I don't typically share solutions, what makes me do that? What effect does it have on the organization?

_____

_____

_____

_____

_____

_____

4. Consider the following:

   • When I communicate with my employees, do I typically talk to them one-on-one or in a group? If I talk to them one-on-one, how do I ensure that my message is consistent from one conversation to the next—particularly if, in the course of these several conversations, I begin to see things slightly differently and my message evolves between conversations.

_____

_____

_____

_____

_____

_____

5. Studies have shown that the way we communicate with our employees and other constituents can have a profound impact on how they feel about the company, about their relationship with you, about their perception of how well the company is performing, and about whether the company's future is bright or not.

   Ask yourself:

   • When I communicate with my employees, either in groups or as individuals, do I show empathy for them?

   • Do I personalize my messaging, or do I take a one-size-fits-all approach?

   • Do I appear to be optimistic and cheerful?

   • Do I recognize them by name?

   • Are my communications timely, or am I often delivering last week's news?

_____

_____

_____

_____

_____

_____

6. When something important happens, how long do you wait before you tell your constituencies? *If your company is publicly traded, there may be regulations concerning when, how, and with whom you share information. Be sure to note this honestly to your employees. Whenever you tell anybody anything, however, one of the first questions that people ask themselves is, "Why did they wait so long to tell me? Why didn't they tell me earlier?" When you can share the information, begin by explaining the delay as a result of the relevant regulation – and don't invoke it as an excuse! Only as an explanation.*

_____

_____

_____

_____

_____

• How do you personally feel when someone tells you about something that affects you greatly and they could have told you earlier than they did?

_____

_____

_____

_____

_____

7. When you share information with your employees, either one-on-one or in groups:

    •   Do you usually tell them "the truth, the whole truth, and nothing but the truth"?

    •   Or do you usually spin it in a way that makes it easier for them to accept?

    •   If so, why?

    •   How do you feel when you find out that a leader has done that to you?

    •   Does it alter your perception of that leader?

    _____

    _____

    _____

    _____

    _____

    _____

8. When you are addressing groups of people:

    •   Do you try to address their hearts?

    •   Or their minds?

    •   What is the difference? Or is there a difference? If there is a difference, is it important

    _____

    _____

    _____

    _____

    _____

    _____

    •   How do you address hearts, as opposed to minds? And vice versa?

    _____

_____

_____

_____

_____

_____

If possible, do a role-play of both approaches regarding both good news—an unexpectedly good quarterly result—and bad news, such as a major quality issue that means you'll miss quarterly forecasts.

9. When you are telling people things, particularly in group settings:

   • Do you illustrate your points with stories?

   • When you are in a group listening to a leader speak, does that leader typically illustrate their points by telling stories?

   • Do stories help leaders make their points clear? If so, how?

   • When do stories detract from a leader's point?

_____

_____

_____

_____

_____

_____

10. Are you a good storyteller? If not, could you learn how to tell stories? Would you want to?

_____

_____

_____

_____

As you can tell, I believe that storytelling is a crucial part of being a leader and building a shared sense of mission and vision with the team. Like leadership, storytelling is a skill that can be taught. Local writing groups often offer such classes; so do course platforms like Coursera (www.coursera.com). They're definitely worth looking into.

CHAPTER 7

IMPLEMENTING CHANGE

If You're Not Going Forward, You Must Be Going Backward.
It's Impossible to Stand Still in a World That's Evolving Around You

1. Imagine that you've been either promoted (from the inside) or hired (from the outside) to head a group of people whose performance—not just individually, but just as importantly, as a group—seems to be far below what you personally believe is possible. What will you do?

_____

_____

_____

_____

_____

Here are some suggestions:

First, spend some time (if you have months, take months), looking and listening carefully, to try to figure out what is wrong and what could be done differently to improve performance. Don't just observe. Ask people in this new group as well. It's likely that many of them have already figured it out, in part or in whole, and are just waiting for someone to ask their opinion. If they offer it, listen but don't judge. You will learn more and earn more respect by listening.

Second, at some point analyze what you've learned. By now, you should have a pretty good idea of who in the group has the most insight. Likely, there are a handful of people who get it. Enlist their help in analyzing the situation. Together, arrive at a "working" (meaning "for the time being") diagnosis of the problem(s) and a set of solutions. This group will function as your "evangelists" going forward.

Third, when you are far enough along and ready, talk to the entire group. Describe the problem. Frame it as *our* problem, not *their* problem. Through your description, try to underscore the urgency of changing how the group is working. Describe how the changes can be made, as well as how much better their performance will be. Most importantly, describe as vividly as you can how much better their (work) lives will be if they can improve their group performance.

Start to implement the changes with a pilot group. Have the pilot group meet regularly to discuss the changes they are implementing and the results that they are getting. Have a few of the evangelists meet with them. Encourage the individual members of the pilot group to express their opinions. Draw them out. Be encouraging, not judgmental.

Remember to protect the pilot group. There will be plenty of people, usually from other parts of the organization, who will find fault with what the pilot group is doing. Try to get their managers to support you and call off the dogs. Improvement almost always requires change, and most people resist change, especially if they are not part of the pilot. It is easier to criticize than to encourage.

When the pilot group is successful, praise them. In appropriate settings, praise the pilot group in front of others in the organization. This must be done, and it must be done carefully. There is a fine line between praising the success of the pilot group in a way that motivates others to want to support the pilot and doing it in a way that engenders jealousy.

If you do this well, in time everyone will want to be part of the pilot. If you do it poorly, everyone who is not part of the pilot will want it to fail and will (even if only subconsciously) sabotage it.

2. Get together in small groups (two or three people) and discuss:

- Why do people resist change?
- Have you ever seen attempts to change fail?
- Find a few concrete examples from your own work experience and describe them to your group.

- What caused these attempts to fail?
- What could have been done differently?

3. With the same group (or shuffle the deck and form new groups), discuss the following:

  - Have you ever seen attempts to change succeed?
  - What caused them to succeed?
  - What can good leaders do to enhance the probability of success?

4. Think about a change that you would like to implement in your own organization.

  - Discuss with your group. How will you go about it?
  - Ask your group to coach you.

This is an easier exercise if you're part of a group that is working through this material in a conscious effort to improve its leadership. But even if you're working on this alone, you can very likely find some like-minded colleagues willing to consider these questions.

CHAPTER 8

LEADING FOR INNOVATION

What We Can Learn from Galileo

Answer the following questions:

1. Are you working? If so, where? If not, where was the last place you worked?

   _____

2. Did you consider the last place you worked to be innovative? Was the leadership itself innovative? Did the leadership encourage the people working there to be innovative? Why do you feel the way you do?

   _____

   _____

   _____

   _____

   _____

3. What motivates you to work hard and accomplish things of value? Are you more motivated by encouragement or by fear?

_____

_____

_____

_____

_____

_____

- Are you more likely to do your best work if your boss tells you he or she thinks that you are capable of it?

_____

- Or are you more likely to do your best work if your boss threatens you with negative repercussions of one sort or another if you fail to accomplish what he or she wants you to?

_____

- When you have a deadline, do you work hard in advance of the deadline in order to have some margin for error, or do you wait until the last minute and let pressure motivate you to finish in time?

_____

- What kind of boss, using what type of approach, does the best job of motivating you? Please describe and explain.

_____

_____

_____

_____

_____

_____

4. Are you more of a conformist or more of a free thinker? What makes you say so?

_____

_____

_____

_____

_____

_____

5. When you try new things, experiment with new approaches, or try to discover/ invent new solutions and they don't work out:

    *   How does your boss respond? With anger or annoyance? Or with praise (for having tried) and encouragement (to keep trying)

    _____

    _____

    _____

    _____

    _____

    _____

    *   How do you feel about their response? Do you think their response is justified? Why, or why not?

    _____

    _____

_____

_____

_____

_____

6. What is your work pattern? Are you a 24/7 kind of person, or do you take time off to relax, reflect, and recoup? Why?

_____

_____

_____

_____

_____

_____

7. Research has shown that the best way to build a culture of innovation is to:

    A. Find good ideas everywhere in the organization—not just at the top, but at all levels.

    B. Motivate people through encouragement and reward, not through punishment and fear.

    C. When you ask someone to try something new, let them have a say in what it will look like and how they will go about creating it.

    D. Insulate them from red tape and rules, and protect them from sabotage.

    E. Give them a feeling of importance. Let them know how important what they are doing may end up being.

    F. Encourage them to take breaks for relaxation, recuperation, and reflection.

    G. If they succeed, reward them. If they fail, praise them for trying and for adding to the knowledge base of the organization,

H. Encourage them to think outside the box. Conformists seldom create new solutions to old problems.

8. How does your management team stack up in comparison with this list?

_____

_____

_____

_____

_____

_____

CASE STUDIES

Let's try our hands at evaluating some well-known leaders. Some of these are known for what they created; others for what they destroyed and how they did so. Yet in each case, they clearly reached the top—at least, for a while. As you read these brief profiles, ask yourself a few questions:

1. What do they seem to do well?
2. What would you criticize them for?
3. Would you like to work in a company that they ran? Why or why not?
4. What lessons do you take from their performance?

These questions are repeated after each case, along with a few that are unique to that situation.

MARC BENIOFF

Chair, Co-CEO, and Cofounder of Salesforce (1999–present)

With a vision of leveraging Salesforce to have a positive impact on the world, Marc Benioff created the 1-1-1 model of philanthropy: Salesforce contributes 1 percent of its equity, 1 percent of its product, and 1 percent of its employees' time back to the community. This idea led to Salesforce's Pledge 1% movement, which helps companies and entrepreneurs worldwide dedicate assets for positive social impact; to date, more than ten thousand businesses in over one hundred countries have generated over $1 billion through this movement. In January 2023, Salesforce announced its plans to lay off 10 percent of its global workforce in response to a broader tech slowdown.

Benioff was named one of the Best-Performing CEOs by *Harvard Business Review*, "Innovator of the Decade" by *Fortune*, and honored by *GLAAD* and the *Billie Jean King Leadership Initiative* for his leadership on equality. He is also the owner and cochair of *TIME* and cofounder of investment firm *TIME Ventures*, is on the *World Economic Forum (WEF)* board of trustees, and he is cofounder of the *WEF Friends of Ocean Action* and *1t.org*—a global movement to conserve and restore one trillion trees. Benioff and his wife, Lynne, focus their philanthropy on public education, health care, homelessness, and the environment.

"This is what ultimately being a chief executive today is going to be about, or really just being a human being on this planet," Benioff said. "You have to follow your heart and follow what you know is right." (https://www.geekwire.com/2020/salesforce-ceo-marc-benioff-offers-leadership-playbook-run-purpose-driven-businesses/)

Related Articles

https://www.salesforce.com/news/stories/how-far-can-the-1-1-1-model-go-this-tech-darling-has-a-unique-approach/

https://www.businessinsider.com/salesforce-ceo-marc-benioff-shares-his-top-communication-tips-2020-12

https://www.forbes.com/sites/forbesleadershipforum/2011/09/14/marc-benioffs-five-leadership-secrets/?sh=47078d1c2534

https://www.geekwire.com/2020/salesforce-ceo-marc-benioff-offers-leadership-playbook-run-purpose-driven-businesses/

https://www.cnbc.com/2020/10/16/salesforce-ceo-marc-benioff-developed-this-mindset-to-lead-in-crisis.html

https://www.inc.com/graham-winfrey/marc-benioff-salesforce-ceo-leadership-lessons-facebook.html

https://news.usc.edu/trojan-family/marc-benioffs-five-life-lessons/

https://www.salesforce.com/company/leadership/bios/bio-benioff/

https://www.yahoo.com/now/salesforces-marc-benioff-named-chief-123200590.html

https://www.reuters.com/technology/salesforce-cut-staff-by-10-close-some-offices-2023-01-04/

Further Reading (may require subscription)

https://www.forbes.com/sites/carminegallo/2020/08/26/the-communication-skills-marc-benioff-says-they-dont-teach-you-in-business-school/?sh=650e98353294

Questions

1. What did Benioff seem to do well?

2. What would you criticize him for?

3. Would you like to work in a company that he ran? Why or why not?

4. What lessons do you take from his performance?

5. Why is vision so important for a leader?

6. Must profitability and philanthropy be mutually exclusive in a business, or can a business thrive when both are pillars of the organization? What kind of impact do you think that outlook has on a company's employees? How can a philanthropic vision be practically implemented in a business?

7. "Communication is the most essential part of my job," Benioff said in an interview. How are good communication skills critical for a leader? How are your communication skills? If there's room for improvement, how will you work on that?

8. If you "follow your heart and follow what you know is right," as Marc Benioff advises, what would you do? What would your vision be as a leader? What steps can you take to get started, and also to plan for the future?

JEFF BEZOS

Founder, President, CEO (1994–2021) and
Executive Chairman (2021–present) of Amazon
Founder, Blue Origin (2000—present)

Jeff Bezos, the founder of Amazon, the revolutionary retailer, and Blue Origin, the space exploration company, is a polarizing figure. As Amazon's founder and CEO, he created a company described as "one of the most influential economic and cultural forces in the world," while also earning a reputation for creating an adversarial corporate culture. While his companies are known for innovation and Amazon for its "customer first" mentality, his autocratic pursuit of success has led warehouse workers to complain that they "would rather go back to a state correctional facility and work for 18 cents an hour" than endure Amazon's close computer-driven performance tracking. "You don't get reported or written up by managers," complained one worker. "You get written up by an algorithm."

Nor have these difficult conditions been confined to warehouses—and, in the case of Blue Origin, they've created measurable performance difficulties. An employee at Blue Origin sent Bezos a memo in 2019 stating, "Our current culture is toxic to our success and many can see it spreading throughout the company." A 2021 article in Bezos-owned *The Washington Post* commented that "the company is rife with sexism, intolerant of employees who dare to contradict their bosses, and lax on safety."

Despite the success of Blue Origin's first crewed mission—the four-person crew included Bezos and his brother—on the fully reusable New Shepherd spacecraft in 2021, organizational dysfunction has created a number of problems. The company's "authoritarian bro culture" affected decision-making and frustrated many employees. The resulting low morale and high turnover has caused significant delays in many programs and hampered competition with Elon Musk's SpaceX.

Much of the blame for this turmoil has been placed on the CEO, Bob Smith, who had been a top executive at Honeywell Aerospace, a massive conglomerate with a distinctly different culture from Blue Origin's. The cultural strife and its resulting performance problems culminated in Blue Origin's loss of a major NASA contract to SpaceX in 2021. As of 2023, Blue Origin still had yet to fly its much-delayed New Glenn rocket, and another rocket engine project had also been plagued with problems. Additional management missteps, including the location of the executive team in a new building rather than mingling them with the front-line staff and a soon-reversed decision to cut the distribution of mission patches to commemorate spaceflights, further strained workforce relations.

During this period, Bezos added to the chaos. Personally distracted by his divorce, he gave Smith free rein at Blue Origin, but occasionally interacted directly with the workforce. In these meetings, Bezos might express interest in an engineering idea for which there was no budget, raising and then dashing hopes. One member of the original Blue Origin executive team noted that his advice for Bezos in 2021 would be "You basically need a new executive team and a totally new culture."[1]

In September 2023, Bezos announced plans to replace Smith by the end of the year. The departures of two additional exeuctives, the senior vice president of operations and the head of research and development, were announced shortly thereafter, along with a plan to restructure the operations department. Whether these changes will correct the clutural challenges that have continued to hamper the company's performance is still an open question.

Related Articles

https://www.msn.com/en-ca/money/companies/bezos-blue-origin-sees-third-executive-departure-amid-restructuring/

https://www.theregister.com/2023/08/03/blue_origin_wfh_rules_change/

https://www.businessinsider.com/jeff-bezos-amazon-leadership-principles-steps-down-andy-jassy-2021-2

https://www.washingtonpost.com/technology/2021/10/11/blue-origin-jeff-bezos-delays-toxic-workplace/

https://www.nytimes.com/2021/09/30/science/jeff-bezos-blue-origin-safety.html

https://www.entrepreneur.com/article/383376

https://www.forbes.com/sites/retailwire/2013/10/22/is-jeff-bezos-a-horrible-boss-and-is-that-good/

https://www.cnbc.com/2019/04/05/amazon-billionaire-ceo-jeff-bezos-ask-yourself-these-12-questions-to-live-a-long-happy-life.html

https://topicinsights.com/leadership-management/jeff-bezos-leadership/

https://www.fingerprintforsuccess.com/blog/jeff-bezos-leadership-style

https://www.theguardian.com/technology/2020/feb/05/amazon-workers-protest-unsafe-grueling-conditions-warehouse

https://www.businessinsider.com/what-you-can-learn-from-jeff-bezos-leadership-style

https://www.theverge.com/2016/4/5/11373438/amazon-corporate-culture-comment-jeff-bezos

https://www.space.com/blue-origin-first-crewed-launch-four-world-records

https://www.reddit.com/r/BlueOrigin/comments/14dyio4/employee_perspective_quality_of_life_destruction/

---

1   Christian Davenport and Rachel Lerman, "Inside Blue Origin," *The Washington Post*, October 11, 2021, https://www.washingtonpost.com/technology/2021/10/11/blue-origin-jeff-bezos-delays-toxic-workplace/

Further Reading (may require subscription or purchase)

https://www.nytimes.com/2015/08/16/technology/inside-amazon-wrestling-big-ideas-in-a-bruising-workplace.html

https://fortune.com/2021/09/30/blue-origin-jeff-bezos-toxic-work-environment-open-letter-ally-abrams-space/

https://research-methodology.net/amazon-organizational-culture-harsh-effectively-contributing-bottom-line-2/

https://hbr.org/2013/10/what-its-like-to-work-for-jeff-bezos-hint-hell-probably-call-you-stupid

Questions

1. What did Bezos seem to do well?

2. What would you criticize him for?

3. Would you like to work in a company that he ran? Why or why not?

4. And, what lessons do you take from his performance?

5. When Jeff Bezos initially thought of the idea for Amazon, he weighed the risks and chose to move ahead. "I didn't think I'd regret trying and failing," Bezos later said. "And I suspected I would always be haunted by a decision not to try at all." Think of some choices you've made in your own life, and also sometimes that you would have liked to try something but didn't. As you look back over your life, what do you find that you regret more: trying and failing at something, or not trying at all? How might you apply your answer to your life and work going forward?

6. Blue Origin's corporate culture has been described by some employees as "authoritarian bro culture," "condescending," "demoralizing," "C-suite out of touch with the employee base," and "dysfunctional, resulting in low morale and high turnover." (https://fortune.com/2021/09/30/blue-origin-jeff-bezos-toxic-work-environment-open-letter-ally-abrams-space/). Have you ever worked in a dysfunctional corporate culture, and if so, how would you describe your experience there? What was the impact of that culture on you and other employees? What could leadership have done to create a more positive culture?

7. How is behavior (both positive and negative) modeled in a culture, and what happens when new employees pick up the kinds of behavior they see in an existing culture?

8. What do you think are Jeff Bezos's strengths and weaknesses as a leader? As an innovator?

9. Jeff Bezos once tweeted: "Listen and be open, but don't let anybody tell you who you are." How do you handle criticism—constructive or otherwise? What are some situations you've been in where people gave you feedback about yourself and

how did you feel about what they had to say and how they delivered it? What are some times where you got some constructive criticism and felt prompted (or not) to change something about yourself?

10. Think about a time when you invented something or came up with a creative solution to a problem. What were the circumstances and how did you feel about your accomplishment? What can you do to increase opportunities for creativity and invention in your own life and work?

ROSALIND "ROZ" BREWER
CEO, Walgreens Boots Alliance (2021–September 2023)

To truly understand the companies she leads Rosalind Brewer makes a point of talking and working with employees at all levels within the organization. "I have some absolute real lived experiences," Brewer said. "When I was at Starbucks I worked the drive-thru window. When I was at Walmart I had three trucks at night so I could learn distribution logistics, warehousing, at those companies. So, I've done the worst and the best of the jobs." (https://hbr.org/2021/12/walgreens-ceo-roz-brewer-to-leaders-put-your-phones-away-and-listen-to-employees)

Dubbed "one of corporate America's most prominent women and Black female executives" by *USA Today* and a "Highly Powerful Woman" by *Forbes* and *Fortune*, Brewer was previously group president and COO of Starbucks, president and CEO of Sam's Club, and held executive positions at Walmart and Kimberly-Clark. She served on the board of directors for Amazon, Lockheed Martin, and Molson Coors Brewing Company, and serves on boards for Westminster School, the Carter Presidential Center, Spelman College, VillageMD, World Business Chicago, the Business Roundtable, and the Smithsonian's National Museum of African-American History and Culture.

Reflecting on recent shifts to remote and hybrid work, and the importance of an organization's culture, Brewer said:

I'm no scientist. I'm not a psychologist, but I will tell you, I've seen time and time again, isolation absolutely never works. . . . We're asking our teams to create opportunities to interact with their organizations twice a week. Come in for lunch or hit the team meeting in person, once a week. The second thing we're doing is thinking about: where are our hubs? Could we have hubs across the United States so that you come in and you feel the culture and you breathe the culture and you live the culture? Because you can't sit on a piece of paper like a strategy can. You can't pull it all off and then go create an action. It's the way you make someone feel, it's the way the environment looks. And then the last thing I would say about driving culture is to be very, very consistent in aligning your decisions with your culture, mission, and values. (https://hbr.org/2021/12/walgreens-ceo-roz-brewer-to-leaders-put-your-phones-away-and-listen-to-employees)

In September 2023, Brewer stepped down, a decision that the company said was mutual. Although she had successfully managed the challenges of the pandemic, including the rollout of the COVID-19 vaccination program at Walgreen's pharmacies, the company had shifted its strategy to focus on the broader U.S. healthcare sector. An industry observer had commented, "While the wisdom of this move is debatable, health care is not Ms. Brewer's forte." (https://www.nytimes.com/2023/09/01/business/rosalind-brewer-walgreens.html)

Related Articles

https://www.cnbc.com/2022/07/26/walgreens-ceo-roz-brewer-on-her-biggest-career-risk.html

https://www.modernhealthcare.com/awards/2022-women-leaders-rosalind-roz-brewer

https://www.cnn.com/2022/06/16/success/black-leadership-juneteenth/index.html

https://blackeoejournal.com/2021/01/walgreens-ceo-roz-brewer-bias-c-suite-youre-black-woman-get-mistaken/

https://www.pharmavoice.com/news/rosalind-brewer-pv100-disrupters/629522/

https://www.usatoday.com/in-depth/opinion/2022/03/22/usa-today-women-year-walgreens-ceo-rosalind-brewer-covid/9290781002/

https://www.forbesmiddleeast.com/leadership/ceo/roz-brewer-on-using-your-power-to-lift-others-were-better-when-we-move-in-herds

https://www.today.com/news/rosalind-brewer-talks-being-black-woman-ceo-today-t217475

https://www.bloomberg.com/features/2016-how-did-i-get-here/rosalind-brewer.html

https://www.businessinsider.com/walgreens-ceo-roz-brewer-reimagine-future-healthcare-transformative-2022-12

Further Reading (may require subscription)

https://www.nytimes.com/2023/09/01/business/rosalind-brewer-walgreens.html

https://hbr.org/2021/12/walgreens-ceo-roz-brewer-to-leaders-put-your-phones-away-and-listen-to-employees

Questions

1. What does Brewer seem to do well?

2. What would you criticize her for?

3. Would you like to work in a company that she ran? Why or why not?

4. And what lessons do you take from her performance?

5. What are some advantages to talking and interacting with people directly, versus texting or emailing them? What types of communications are best done in person in an organization?

6. What's one of the biggest risks you ever took as a leader or in a job/organization? How did it turn out? Did you question your decision along the way or trust your gut/intuition? What's the best way to handle it if you or an employee take a risk and it's not successful? What's the value in trying and owning an unsuccessful attempt?

7. Roz Brewer said: "One of the things that I think about when I'm thinking about diversity is diversity of thought. Because we can also realize that there are individuals who may not be of diverse culture, race, or gender themselves, but where is their mindset? How do they think about different cultures and different environments?" (https://hbr.org/2021/12/walgreens-ceo-roz-brewer-to-leaders-put-your-phones-away-and-listen-to-employees). What does diversity and inclusion mean to you? How do teams and organizational cultures benefit when people of different backgrounds and mindsets work together?

CARLY FIORINA
CEO, Hewlett-Packard (1999–2005)

Carly Fiorina—once described as a "one-woman wrecking crew during her tenure as CEO of Hewlett-Packard" (https://www.sfchronicle.com/opinion/openforum/article/Fiorina-had-that-job-killing-touch-6527942.php)—is one of the most controversial leaders in tech history. While some point to an increase in revenue as proof of her success (during her tenure, revenue growth and cash flow increased by 4x, but profits fell), critics argue that HP's disastrous slide (the share price fell by 60 percent, from $52 per share to $21 per share) resulted directly from Fiorina's misjudgment of the PC market, poor assessment of her ability to run HP and manage its dysfunctional board, and—at heart—a failure of leadership on multiple levels, including her failure to grant significant recognition to the old "HP Way" culture established by founders Bill Hewlett and David Packard.

As HP's CEO, Fiorina modeled a drastic change in culture, which included mass layoffs, callousness toward employees, and a kind of dog-eat-dog mentality. Once known for its creative, collaborative, respectful culture, HP under Fiorina's leadership came to represent a toxic, internally competitive, highly corporate climate that lost many of its best employees (along with billions of dollars). Acquiring Compaq Computer Corporation—an "old tech" hardware company—instead of expanding into a more promising future of software and services as other tech giants were doing at the time, is widely considered to be one of Fiorina's most disastrous decisions.

Related Articles

https://www.pbs.org/newshour/economy/fiorinas-career-tech-ceo-still-matter-debate
https://digitalcommons.georgefox.edu/cgi/viewcontent.cgi?article=1065&context=gfsb

https://www.sfchronicle.com/opinion/openforum/article/Fiorina-had-that-job-killing-touch-6527942.php

https://www.oregonlive.com/opinion/2015/05/a_closer_look_at_carly_fiorina.html

https://www.cnet.com/tech/tech-industry/hps-carly-fiorina-era-is-finally-over-good-riddance/

https://www.pbs.org/newshour/economy/fiorinas-career-tech-ceo-still-matter-debate

https://www.politico.com/magazine/story/2015/09/carly-fiorina-ceo-jeffrey-sonnenfeld-2016-213163/

https://calaborfed.org/carly_fiorina_job_killer_extraordinaire/

Further Reading (may require subscription)

https://www.nytimes.com/2015/09/18/upshot/fiorina-grew-hewlett-packards-sales-but-not-its-profits.html

https://www.nytimes.com/2015/09/27/opinion/carly-fiorina-really-was-that-bad.html

https://www.forbes.com/sites/nomiprins/2015/05/05/carly-fiorinas-judgment-problem/

Questions

1. What did Fiorina seem to do well?

2. What would you criticize her for?

3. Would you like to work in a company that she ran? Why or why not?

4. What lessons do you take from her performance?

5. Do you think that being the first female CEO in a world of "tech bros" may have impacted her leadership style and behavior? If so, how?

ELIZABETH HOLMES
Founder and CEO, Theranos (2003–2018)

In 2003, Elizabeth Holmes founded Theranos: a seemingly revolutionary start-up built around the concept of using proprietary technology to yield extensive medical test results, including detection of cancer and high cholesterol, from just a pinprick amount of blood. For over a decade, Theranos and its charismatic, media-savvy CEO generated dazzling levels of excitement, publicity, and investment capital, until a 2015 *Wall Street Journal* article alleged fraudulent practices. This prompted the Department of Justice, the Securities and Exchange Commission, and the Centers for Medicare and Medicaid Services to launch civil and criminal inquiries into the company's blood testing services. Within three years, Theranos had dissolved. After an extensive trail, both Holmes and her co-founder, former romantic partner, and president, Ramesh "Sunny" Balwani, were convincted of fraud and other charges. On May 30, 2023, Holmes—now the mother of two who still claims she was just a "hard-driving young CEO who ... quickly got in over her head" under the burden of investor expectations—reported to prison for an 11-year term. With good behavior, she is likely to be released in 2032.

Related Articles

https://news.miami.edu/stories/2021/09/theranos-trial-highlights-the-dark-side-of-leadership.html

https://www.psychologytoday.com/us/blog/the-leader-within/202203/how-do-destructive-leaders-attract-followers

https://www.entrepreneur.com/article/424934

https://timesofindia.indiatimes.com/blogs/innovate-or-die/all-leaders-should-pay-attention-to-the-case-of-holmes-not-sherlock-the-other-one/

https://www.bbc.com/news/business-58336998

https://www.cnn.com/2022/11/18/tech/elizabeth-holmes-theranos-sentencing/index.html

https://www.npr.org/2023/05/30/1178728092/elizabeth-holmes-prison-sentence-theranos-fraud-silicon-valley

https://apnews.com/article/elizabeth-holmes-theranos-prison-early-release-537ea5a5b9f9bed735a9f62a7a4dfb07

Further Reading (may require subscription)

https://www.forbes.com/sites/lindsaykohler/2022/01/04/what-the-elizabeth-holmes-verdict-teaches-us-about-psychological-safety-at-work/

https://www.bloomberg.com/news/articles/2022-01-05/what-can-we-learn-from-the-trial-of-theranos-ceo-elizabeth-holmes

Questions

1. What do Holmes seem to do well?

2. What would you criticize her for?

3. Would you like to work in a company that she ran? Why or why not?

4. What lessons do you take from her performance?

5. Elizabeth Holmes worked to develop a positive brand image, in many ways modeling herself after Steve Jobs, even to the point of wearing wearing a signature black turtleneck and copying some of his less-attractive behaviors. What similarities and differences do you see between these two CEOs? Do you think it's helpful for aspiring leaders to model themselves after famous CEOs? Why or why not?

6. In the case of Theranos, medical laboratory test results were being falsified for profit. What responsibility does a leader have regarding the public trust? What should a leader do in situations where ethics and profit do not align?

7. What is confirmation bias? What role did it play in the downfall of Theranos? As a leader, what steps can you take to recognize and avoid confirmation bias?

TRAVIS KALANICK
Cofounder and CEO, Uber (2009–2017)

Amid a whirlwind of public reports about unethical corporate culture—and a few emotional meltdowns—Uber's "brash, take no prisoners" tech bro CEO Travis Kalanick resigned after major shareholders demanded new leadership. The ride-hailing service that transformed the global transportation industry became an example of Silicon Valley start-up culture gone wrong, with accusations of a workplace culture that included discrimination, sexual harassment, and questionable ethical and business practices. An embarrassing video of Kalanick berating an Uber driver illustrated a variety of issues that were widely discussed at the time: not only Kalanick's apparent deficiencies in effective communication and listening, but a corporate tone set from the top that modeled arrogance and a lack of accountability.

One journalist described Kalanick's momentous rise and fall this way: "The strategies that brought the business its first brushes of success became more damaging than helpful, and there was a lack of personal accountability that would have allowed Kalanick to realize that."[2]

Kalanick's replacement, Dara Khosrowshahi, joined the company in August 2017. When the company struggled with a shortage of drivers in September 2022, he went undercover as one—"Dave K."—to understand the challenges they faced. His experience produced four significant changes that made the drivers' experiences safer and more profitable, boosting Uber's market share by 12 percentage points between 2020 and 2022 and helping the company generate its first adjusted annual profit. By comparison, Lyft's market share fell by 14 percentage points over the same period.[3]

Related Articles

https://www.inc.com/minda-zetlin/7-leadership-lessons-you-can-learn-from-travis-kalanicks-response-to-ubers-cultu.html

https://www.inc.com/susan-steinbrecher/ubers-travis-kalanick-its-time-to-grow-up-as-a-leader.html

https://www.foxbusiness.com/features/uber-ceo-travis-kalanicks-leadership-problem

https://www.entrepreneur.com/business-news/travis-kalanicks-downfall-shows-how-necessary/307774

https://www.cnbc.com/2017/06/12/the-biggest-mistake-that-ceos-like-ubers-travis-kalanick-make-commentary.html

https://www.bbc.com/news/technology-40352868

https://www.bloomberg.com/news/newsletters/2022-07-14/uber-travis-kalanick-was-a-leader-for-a-very-different-tech-era

https://www.theguardian.com/technology/2017/mar/07/uber-work-culture-travis-kalanick-susan-fowler-controversy

---

2   Nina Zipkin, "Travis Kalanick's Downfall Shows How Necessary Accountability is to Strong Leadership," *Entrepreneur*, January 19, 2018, https://www.entrepreneur.com/business-news/travis-kalanicks-downfall-shows-how-necessary/307774)

3   Peter Cohan, "4 Leadership Lessons from Uber's Undercover CEO," *Inc.com*, April 19, 2023, https://www.inc.com/peter-cohan/4-leadership-lessons-from-ubers-undercover-ceole.html

https://www.pbs.org/newshour/economy/column-travis-kalanicks-downfall-cost-toxic-bro-culture

Further Reading (may require subscription)

https://www.nytimes.com/2017/06/21/technology/uber-ceo-travis-kalanick.html

https://www.vanityfair.com/news/2019/08/behind-the-epic-meltdown-that-ended-travis-kalanick

Questions

1. What did Kalanick seem to do well?

2. What would you criticize him for?

3. Would you like to work in a company that he ran? Why or why not?

4. And what lessons do you take from his performance?

5. How much can changing a company's leadership change a company's culture? How does that happen, and how quickly do you think culture change can occur when a new leader models different behavior?

6. What is the effect of lack of accountability, or "passing the buck," on an organization's culture and employees? Internally, and also externally, in terms of shareholder and public perception of a company?

7. What is emotional intelligence (EQ), and why is it important in a leader? Did Travis Kalanick display EQ—why or why not? If the top goals of a company are growing and winning, how can that mindset lead to deprioritizing other values critical to positive corporate culture? What is the effect of this over time?

ADAM NEUMANN

Founder and CEO, We Work/The We Company (2010-2019)

In 2010, Adam Neumann founded what became the We Company. At the time, WeWork was an office-space colocation company. An entrepreneur could rent as little as one desk and have access to a copier, IT services, a kitchen, and even a conference room. WeWork's then-innovative model rode the entrepreneurial wave, filling the demand for flexible office space and serving the needs of companies from start-ups to Fortune 500 giants. At its peak, the company had space in more than 110 cities and 29 countries, and was valued at $47 billion.

Neumann, famous for his charm and confidence, generated a lot of that value. He portrayed himself as a tech visionary even though, commented one critic, "he was just leasing office space."[4] In 2014, Neumann reorganized the company to give his Series B and C shares 20 times the votes of those belonging to other investors. Stories abounded of the "frat-boy culture" that Neumann led, along with his self-indulgent antics and abusive expectations of staff. Sexual harassment and age discrimination lawsuits followed. Eventually, the company tried to go public, only to find that public investors were less than thrilled with its high-loss model. The company's valuation collapsed to $10 billion and then $4 billion and SoftBank, a major investor, forced Neumann to resign in 2019.

In the aftermath of Neumann's hubris, self-dealing (the company rented office space in buildings that Neumann owned), and nepotism (Neumann hired his wife as Chief Brand Officer despite her complete lack of relevant experience), it's easy to lose sight of his accomplishments: he "fundamentally redesigned the office experience and led a paradigm-changing global company."[5] Known for his imagination, audacious ideas, and sweeping claims,[6] Neumann needed a group of adults to either keep him focused on the daily work of growing the company or to ringfence him while they took care of the daily work. In backing Neumann's new residential real estate company in 2022, Marc Andreessen of Andreessen Horowitz said, "We love seeing repeat-founders build on past successes but growing from lessons learned." One might wonder to what extent Neumann has learned his lessons.

Related Articles

https://www.leadershipdynamics.io/insights-and-impact/adam-neumann-can-be-a-great-ceo-but-he-needs-the-right-team-around-him

https://www.vox.com/recode/2019/9/23/20879656/wework-mess-explained-ipo-softbank

https://www.dailymail.co.uk/news/article-8860017/How-Partyer-Chief-WeWork-founder-Adam-Neumann-tequila-fueled-leadership-style.html

Marc Andreessen, "Investing in Flow," Andreessen Horowitz website, August 15, 2022, cited in Lerner & Leamon, *VC, PE, and the Financing of Entrepreneurship*, (J. Wiley, 2023), p. 81.

https://www.businessinsider.com/lessons-leaders-learn-fall-wework-ceo-adam-neumann-millennial-success-coach#-lesson-2-lead-with-a-strategic-plan-first-insert-radical-ideas-second-2

Questions

1. What did Neumann seem to do well?

2. What would you criticize him for?

---

4   https://www.dailymail.co.uk/news/article-8860017/How-Partyer-Chief-WeWork-founder-Adam-Neumann-tequila-fueled-leadership-style.html

5   Marc Andreessen, "Investing in Flow," Andreessen Horowitz website, August 15, 2022, cited in Lerner & Leamon, *VC, PE, and the Financing of Entrepreneurship*, (J. Wiley, 2023), p. 81.

6   https://www.businessinsider.com/lessons-leaders-learn-fall-wework-ceo-adam-neumann-millennial-success-coach#lesson-2-lead-with-a-strategic-plan-first-insert-radical-ideas-second-2

3. Would you like to work in a company that he ran? Why or why not?

4. What lessons do you take from his performance?

5. If you had been invested in WeWork, how would you have managed Neumann? Would you have allowed him to invest the B and C shares with so much power? How would you have prevented him from doing so?

6. There is an old saying "power corrupts. Absolute power corrupts absolutely." Yet an innovative and successful founder can deservedly claim they deserve the perks of their success. How would you want that dilemma balanced in a company you founded?

JEFF SKILLING

Enron (1990-2001)

Enron was a Wall Street darling. The management team was known as the "smartest guys in the room." Until it wasn't and they weren't and the company collapsed in what was at that time the largest bankruptcy filing in U.S. history on December 2, 2001. While Ken Lay was the CEO through much of Enron's existence, Jeffrey Skilling, a former McKinsey consultant, was the mastermind behind the company's success and subsequent downfall.

Skilling was the consultant who helped transform a stodgy gas supplier into a hotshot trading company. He hired "the best and brightest" traders, offering them a list of perks akin to any Silicon Valley start-up in exchange for a grueling work schedule. The internal culture focused on profits, despite the stated adherence to "Enron values of respect, integrity, communication, and excellence (RICE)." Everyone in the organization was intensely focused on doing deals and posting earnings. Employees competed fiercely and valued immediate success above long-term potential growth. The company became obsessed with secrecy in its trading contracts and its financial disclosures, and the staff tried to curry favor with managers. The culture was termed a "pressure cooker." One annual report said, "When Enron no longer needs someone, they are removed and replaced. We insist on results."

But as the economy stumbled in 2000, the complex financial instruments that Skilling and CFO Andrew Fastow had developed became increasingly shaky. An obscure footnote triggered questions from accounting experts that Skilling replied to with dismissal and antagonism. Skilling took over as CEO in early 2001, only to resign six months later as more questions circled around Enron's accounting. In December 2001, the company collapsed into bankruptcy.

Most of the Enron executive team went to prison, apart from two who died first. Skilling completed a 12-year prison term in 2019. Fastow made a plea deal and served five years in prison. Many employees, though, lost their jobs and their life savings—their 401-Ks were packed with Enron stock.

Related articles

https://www.journalofaccountancy.com/issues/2002/apr/theriseandfallofenron.html

https://www.washingtonpost.com/archive/politics/2002/01/27/enrons-culture-fed-its-demise/d73cf80c-0d00-4281-848d-968683828ef9/

https://www.cnbc.com/2021/12/02/enrons-executives-became-household-names-heres-where-they-are-now.html

https://www.epi.org/publication/issuebriefs_ib174/

https://legacy.npr.org/news/specials/enron/employees.html#:~:text=Many%20of%20those%20workers%20were,investment%20accounts%20depleted%20or%20destroyed.

Questions

1. What did Skilling seem to do well?

2. What would you criticize him for?

3. Some people loved working in Enron. What elements of the culture seem appealing? Would you like to work in a company that Skilling ran? Why or why not?

4. What lessons do you take from his performance?

5. The top three risk factors associated with management fraud as outlined in SAS 82 are: "unduly aggressive earnings targets and management bonus compensation based on those target; excessive interest by management in maintaining stock price or earnings trend through the use of unusually aggressive accounting practices; and management setting unduly aggressive financial targets and expectations for operating personnel." How can you set up a culture to mitigate these risk factors?

6. Business school classmates of Skilling say that even then, he had a passion for succeeding regardless of the means he used to do it. How can you change someone like that? Is it even possible?

VOLODYMYR ZELENSKY
President of Ukraine (2019–present)

"The fight is here; I need ammunition, not a ride," said President Volodymyr Zelensky, when the US government offered to evacuate him and his family to safety shortly after Russia attacked Ukraine in February 2022.[7] His response went viral. The world had assumed that Russia's

---

7   Sharon Braithwaite, "Zelensky Refuses U.S. Offer to Evacuate," *CNN*.Com, February 26, 2022, https://www.cnn.com/2022/02/26/europe/ukraine-zelensky-evacuation-intl/index.html

illegal invasion of Ukraine would be brief and unstoppable. Now it sat up and took notice. This scrappy comedic actor-turned-president and the people of Ukraine were pushing back against a global bully. Here, it seemed, was David facing Goliath.

President Zelensky knew he was a prime target for Russian forces in the war, yet from the beginning he made himself visible: sharing videos of meetings and meals with troops, openly visiting cities throughout Ukraine, and using digital technology and his skills as a performer to maximum effect to inspire and communicate with world leaders and populations, as well as his own people. Winston Churchill references began to fly. Popular leaders—from Ronald Reagan to fictional captain Jason Nesmith from the movie *Galaxy Quest*—were invoked. And then something began to happen. The small, democratic, seemingly outmatched country of Ukraine began to win battles. Ukrainian troops liberated occupied territories, vowing to push on through the harsh winter and take the fight to Moscow itself.

At the date of writing, the outcome of the war is unknown. But the leadership and courage modeled by President Zelensky and the spirit of the Ukrainian people have already earned their place in history. As this president—with the spirit he embodies—and his people work together to fight for democracy and independence, home and country, isn't that what true leadership is all about? As President Zelensky leads his country in standing up for something noble in the face of an autocratic bully, we see in real time how effective true leadership can be in advancing the power of good in a sometimes cynical and weary world. As *TIME* explained: "For proving that courage can be as contagious as fear, for stirring people and nations to come together in defense of freedom, for reminding the world of the fragility of democracy—and of peace—Volodymyr Zelensky and the spirit of Ukraine are TIME's 2022 Person of the Year."[8]

Related Articles

https://time.com/person-of-the-year-2022-volodymyr-zelensky-ukraine-choice/

https://news.yahoo.com/volodymyr-zelensky-pays-tribute-freedom-024225122.html

https://www.cnn.com/2022/03/08/politics/zelensky-ukraine-churchill-what-matters/index.html

https://www.washingtonpost.com/tv/2022/12/09/david-letterman-interview-zelensky/

https://insight.kellogg.northwestern.edu/newsletters/what-makes-zelensky-such-a-strong-leader

https://www.rd.com/article/volodymyr-zelensky-leadership/

https://knowledge.wharton.upenn.edu/article/what-can-leaders-learn-from-ukraines-volodymyr-zelenskyy/

https://bigthink.com/the-present/virtue-crisis-leadership-zelenskyy/

https://news.harvard.edu/gazette/story/2022/09/be-unstoppable-be-true-to-yourself-but-be-just/

https://www.buffalo.edu/ubnow/stories/2022/03/tesluk-zelensky-servant-leadership.html

https://www.businessinsider.com/president-zelenskyys-unadorned-strategy-is-the-future-of-crisis-leadership-2022-3

https://www.theatlantic.com/podcasts/archive/2022/09/meeting-zelensky/671369/

---

8   Edward Felsenthal, "Volodymyr Zelensky and the Spritir of Ukraine," *Time Magazine,* December 7, 2022, https://time.com/person-of-the-year-2022-volodymyr-zelensky-ukraine-choice/.

https://www.journalofdemocracy.org/articles/how-zelensky-has-changed-ukraine/

https://www.axios.com/2022/03/15/volodymyr-zelensky-ukraine-leadership-courage

https://leaders.com/articles/leadership/volodymyr-zelensky/

https://www.nbcnews.com/news/world/volodymyr-zelenskyy-become-global-phenomenon-rcna24355

https://www.raconteur.net/war-in-ukraine-leading-through-crisis/what-business-leaders-can-learn-from-ukraines-zelensky/

https://www.linkedin.com/pulse/zelensky-effect-inspirational-leaders-impact-followers-jones

Further Reading (may require subscription)

https://www.washingtonpost.com/opinions/2022/11/23/zelensky-resistance-ukraine-war/

https://www.forbes.com/sites/forbesbooksauthors/2022/05/18/how-ukraines-president-demonstrated-historic-servant-leadership/

Questions

1. What does Zelensky seem to do well?

2. What would you criticize him for?

3. Would you like to work in a company that he ran? Why or why not?

4. What lessons do you take from his performance?

5. Are emotions contagious? How so? What is the effect on a population or organization when a leader models courage and sticking together versus fear and every man for himself? As a leader, how can modeling courage and responsibility inspire others to do the same? What is a leader's responsibility to their followers in the face of threat?

6. What is the value of a sense of humor and shared laughter in leadership? What are some examples of this? Do you believe there is power in comedy, satire, and laughter? Why or why not?

7. After interviewing President Zelensky, David Letterman explained: "[Zelensky] said, 'I'm not brave, I'm responsible.' And that's an excellent way of putting what people are doing. We're not laughing about this. We're taking care of business and we're prevailing, for heaven's sakes."[9] What do you think about that statement? As a leader, is there a difference between bravery and responsibility in a time of crisis? Explain your thoughts on this.

---

9   Geoff Edgers, "David Letterman on His Surprise Ukraine Trip and Zelensky Interview," The Washington Post,, December 9, 2022, https://www.washingtonpost.com/tv/2022/12/09/david-letterman-interview-zelensky/)

EXAMPLES OF THE 150 VALUE

- Accepting
- Accountabilty
- Acknowledgment
- Adaptability
- Affection
- Altruism
- Ambition
- Appreciative
- Articulate
- Authenticity
- Awareness
- Benevolence
- Bravery
- Calmness
- Caring
- Cheerfulness
- Civic-minded
- Collaboration
- Compassionate
- Competence
- Compromise-builder
- Confidence
- Connectedness
- Consideration
- Consistency
- Content

- Contribution
- Cooperation
- Courage
- Courtesy
- Creativity
- Curiosity
- Decorum
- Dedication
- Dependability
- Determination
- Diligence
- Diplomacy
- Discernment
- Discretion
- Diversity
- Driven
- Educated
- Empathic
- Empowering
- Energetic
- Enthusiasm
- Environmental consciousness
- Equanimity
- Excelling
- Expertise

- Even-temper
- Fact-based
- Fairness
- Fidelity
- Flexibility
- Foresighted
- Forgiveness
- Fortitude
- Friendliness
- Frugality
- Generosity
- Gentleness
- Goal-oriented
- Good communication
- Good judgment
- Good manners
- Good sportsmanship
- Gracious ness
- Gratitude
- Gravitas
- Honest
- Hopeful
- Humble
- Humor
- Inclusiveness
- Independence

- Industriousness
- Initiative
- Inner peace
- Innovation
- Inquisitive
- Integrity
- Joyous
- Justice
- Kindness
- Knowledge
- Listening
- Loyalty
- Magnaminity
- Maturity
- Modesty
- Multi-dimensional
- Negotiator
- Networked
- Nurturing
- Obedience
- Open-hearted
- Open-minded
- Optimism
- Organization
- Patience
- Peacefulness
- Perseverance
- Persistence
- Politeness
- Pragmatism
- Problem-solving
- Prudence
- Punctuality
- Rationality

- Realistic
- Reasonability
- Reliability
- Researcher
- Resilience
- Resourcefulness
- Respect
- Responsibility
- Responsiveness
- Secure
- Self-acceptance
- Self-activaion
- Self-awareness
- Self-control
- Self-discipline
- Selflessness
- Self-reliance
- Sensitivity
- Serenity
- Seriousness
- Sharing
- Sincerity
- Skill
- Steadfast
- Sympathy
- Tact
- Teamwork
- Tenacity
- Thoughtfulness
- Time management
- Tolerance
- Tranquility
- Transparency
- Trust

- Truthfulness
- Understanding
- Unselfishness
- Warmth
- Well-read
- Wide-ranging
- Willingness to Listen

Good Luck on your Management Journey,

wherever it takes you!

www.ingramcontent.com/pod-product-compliance
Lightning Source LLC
Chambersburg PA
CBHW051414200326
41520CB00023B/7234